DRAGSTERS

Big Buddy BOOKS
Amazing Vehicles

Sarah Tieck

ABDO
Publishing Company

Amazing Vehicles

VISIT US AT
www.abdopublishing.com

Published by ABDO Publishing Company, 8000 West 78th Street, Edina, Minnesota 55439.

Copyright © 2011 by Abdo Consulting Group, Inc. International copyrights reserved in all countries. No part of this book may be reproduced in any form without written permission from the publisher. Big Buddy Books™ is a trademark and logo of ABDO Publishing Company.

Printed in the United States of America, North Mankato, Minnesota.
102010
012011

  PRINTED ON RECYCLED PAPER

Coordinating Series Editor: Rochelle Baltzer
Contributing Editors: Megan M. Gunderson, BreAnn Rumsch, Marcia Zappa
Graphic Design: Deb Coldiron, Maria Hosley, Marcia Zappa
Cover Photograph: *iStockphoto*: ©iStockphoto.com/rcyoung.
Interior Photographs/Illustrations: *AP Photo*: Auto Imagery (p. 29), Auto Imagery, Inc., NHRA (p. 25), Ellis R. Bosworth (p. 29), Ric Francis (p. 27), Greg Griffo/The Indianapolis Star (p. 21), Kelly Humphrey/Brainerd Dispatch (p. 9), John Leyba/The Denver Post (p. 7), Ben Margot (pp. 5, 17), National Hotrod Racing Association (p. 15); *Getty Images*: Allan Grant/Time Life Pictures (p. 30); *iStockphoto*: ©iStockphoto.com/rcyoung (pp. 10, 14, 20, 28); *Shutterstock*: Mike Brake (p. 19), Raymond den Haan (p. 13), Christopher Halloran (p. 23), Marcy J. Levinson (p. 23), Juerg Schreiter (p. 25), Derek Yegan (p. 11).

Library of Congress Cataloging-in-Publication Data

Tieck, Sarah, 1976-
  Dragsters / Sarah Tieck.
    p. cm. -- (Amazing vehicles)
  ISBN 978-1-61714-696-1
  1. Dragsters--Juvenile literature. I. Title.
  TL236.2.T54 2011
  629.228--dc22
                            2010031070

CONTENTS

It can be very hot inside a dragster! But, the car is built to protect the driver from the engine heat.

GET MOVING

Imagine sitting behind the wheel of a dragster. The engine roars. As the tires spin, smoke fills the air. The light turns green, and the race starts! You let off the brakes and **accelerate** to the finish line.

Have you ever looked closely at a dragster? Many parts work together to make it move. A dragster is an amazing vehicle!

WHAT IS A DRAGSTER?

Dragsters are the fastest race cars in the world. They have powerful engines. They may go hundreds of miles per hour in just a few seconds. They race on straight tracks called drag strips.

Drag races last just 5 to 15 seconds. Speeds range from 100 miles (160 km) to more than 300 miles (480 km) per hour.

7

A CLOSER LOOK

A dragster is **designed** for speed! Its smooth body is shaped to help it move quickly. And, it is made to keep the driver safe at high speeds.

A dragster's body is built on a strong frame. It has many of the same parts as standard cars. But, the parts are built differently. The tires, engine, and controls are made to be light, but strong.

DRAGSTERS

8

 3

 2

 1

4

GEICO Powersports

LUCAS OIL

GEICO Powersports

LUCAS OIL PRODUCTS

 4

1 The **tires** are called slicks. They have smooth, soft surfaces. This helps the dragster grip the track.

2 The **engine** is usually behind the driver. But, sometimes it is in front.

3 Dragsters often have **wings** on the rear and the front. They help keep the car's tires on the track.

4 The dragster's **body** is often painted with sponsor names and signs. This helps companies and groups gain attention.

FAST FACT: Dragsters are expensive. They may cost more than $100,000 to build. And, fuel for one race may cost $400 or more!

TUNE-UP

Much thought goes into building a dragster. First, people plan the **design**. Then, they order special parts and begin building the dragster.

Once the parts are put together, the dragster is painted. Designers often choose bright colors or patterns. Sometimes, **sponsors** also have their names painted on the dragster.

Teams of people work on dragsters. They make sure the cars are in top condition for races.

A dragster races fast because of its powerful engine. Still, a drag race is very hard on the engine. So, most of its parts have a limited life. The engine must be rebuilt between races.

Dragster engines are made up of many working parts. It takes about 75 minutes for a team to take apart and rebuild some engines.

13

TOP FUEL CARS

There are more than 200 types of vehicles called dragsters. When most people think of dragsters, they picture top **fuel** or top alcohol cars.

Top fuel and top alcohol cars are long and narrow. The engine is behind the driver's seat. A large rear wing and a smaller front wing help keep the car on the ground.

Top fuel cars use nitromethane. This fuel creates more energy than the fuel used in most racing cars.

STOCK CARS

Stock cars are another popular type of dragster. They look like cars you might see on a highway. And like those standard cars, stock cars use gasoline as **fuel**.

Some stock cars are built from standard cars. But, their insides are made for racing. They can reach speeds of 200 miles (320 km) per hour in less than seven seconds!

Horsepower is a way to measure an engine's power. Some types of stock car engines have about 1,200 horsepower. That is about eight times more powerful than a standard car!

FUNNY CARS

Funny cars are also popular dragsters. They look similar to stock cars. But, they use the same **fuel** as top fuel cars.

Funny cars got their name because of their looks. They have wheels that are farther forward than most stock cars. And, they have a very light frame called a tube frame. These features help the car **accelerate** better.

The doors of many funny cars don't open. So, drivers must climb in through the windows.

FAST FACT: Junior drag racers are as young as eight! They have special licenses.

THE DRIVER'S SEAT

Dragsters are fun and exciting to drive. But, they can also be unsafe. It takes practice and skill to drive them safely.

Only racers drive dragsters. They have driver's **licenses**. And, most are **professionals** who are trained to safely handle high speeds.

Drivers wear special gear to stay safe. This includes a helmet, boots, and gloves. And, their clothes may protect them from fire.

AT THE TRACK

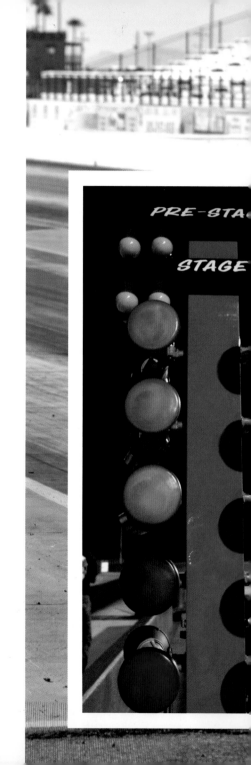

Most dragsters race on straight tracks that are one-fourth mile (0.4 km) long. The drag strip usually has at least two lanes.

The center of the lane is called the groove. The groove is a path of rubber left by other cars on the track surface. In the groove, cars can gain **traction** quicker and run faster times.

A light pole called the Christmas tree tells the drivers when to go. The yellow lights mean wait. The green lights mean go. And, the red lights mean someone started too soon.

23

Each race is called a pass. Two dragsters start side by side at the starting line. When the light turns green, drivers **accelerate** as fast as they can.

When drivers pass the finish line, they slow down. It may take more space for them to slow down than the race took!

The losing car is out of the race. The winner goes on to the next round. Rounds continue until there is just one driver left. That driver wins the whole race!

Some dragsters have parachutes to help them slow down.

Before a drag race, drivers do a burnout. They spin their tires in water to get them hot and clean. This helps the tires grip the track better.

FAMOUS RACERS

Men and women race dragsters. John Force is a famous funny car racer. He has won 125 national races. He is in the Motorsports Hall of Fame of America.

Don Garlits is a well-known top **fuel** car racer. He has won 144 national races. Garlits changed the **design** of the top fuel car after his engine exploded in 1970. He put the engine in back. This change caught on because it kept drivers safer.

John Force (*below*) and his daughter Ashley (*right*) raced at the 2008 Summit Southern Nationals in Atlanta, Georgia. Ashley won!

27

PAST TO PRESENT

In the 1930s, some people rebuilt old cars and gave them powerful engines. These light, fast cars became known as hot rods. Drivers would race them on streets.

Today, people still race fast cars. But, the cars are called dragsters, and the races happen on racetracks. **Sponsors** and teams of trained workers are behind these powerful cars. Dragsters are amazing vehicles!

Many early hot rods (*above*) were standard cars changed to move fast. Today's dragsters (*left*) have improved designs and more power.

BLAST FROM THE PAST

Early hot rod races on public streets caused many crashes. A man named Wally Parks loved hot rods and racing. But, he wanted to make it safe. He organized races on old airport runways and other off-street places.

In 1951, Parks and other hot rod fans formed the NHRA to make races safer. The first official NHRA race was in 1953. Over the years, the NHRA made rules. In time, hot rod racing became an official sport.

Wally Parks

IMPORTANT WORDS

accelerate (ihk-SEH-luh-rayt) to increase speed.

design (dih-ZINE) to make a plan. A designer is a person who has ideas and works on making a plan.

fuel (FYOOL) something burned to give heat or power.

license (LEYE-suhnts) a paper or a card showing that someone is allowed to do something by law.

professional (pruh-FEHSH-nuhl) a person who works for money rather than for pleasure.

sponsor a person or a group that agrees to pay expenses for the activities of another person or group.

traction (TRAK-shuhn) the power to hold onto a surface without slipping while moving.

WEB SITES

To learn more about dragsters, visit ABDO Publishing Company online. Web sites about dragsters are featured on our Book Links page. These links are routinely monitored and updated to provide the most current information available.

www.abdopublishing.com

INDEX